A
Gift from
GRACE TO YOU
2006

www.gty.org

JOHN MACARTHUR

God's Gift of
CHRISTMAS

NASHVILLE, TENNESSEE

THE WORD BECAME FLESH,

AND DWELT AMONG US, AND WE SAW HIS GLORY,

GLORY AS OF THE ONLY BEGOTTEN FROM THE FATHER,

FULL OF GRACE AND TRUTH.

—John 1:14

"HE WHO HAS SEEN ME HAS SEEN THE FATHER."

—John 14:9

THE BIRTH OF HOPE

Christmas is a time of celebration and song, goodwill and good food, family and friends. But it's important to remember that the source of Christmas is the saving Christ.

Humanity is lost, fallen. We were separated from God because of our sin, and our only hope of forgiveness was for someone completely innocent of any wrongdoing to take all the punishment for our crimes. Such a perfect life and a perfect love were impossible for any human to achieve, so God Himself did it for us. He sent His Son from eternity into mortality, from glory into flesh, and from a throne to a manger. Ultimate hope was born in ultimate humility.

Whenever you study the Gospels, you see God in every picture of Christ. He talks like God, acts like God, thinks like God, performs miracles that only God could do, teaches truth only God would teach, and responds with the love, goodness, wisdom, and omniscience that only God could possess. And it all begins with the birth of the divine Child.

This is the immeasurable gift of Christmas. Christ, God's own Son, gave up His wealth and privilege to live as God with us, Immanuel, that He might save His people from our sins and that through His poverty we might become rich.

The miraculous gift of Christmas is God being born in a manger, so we can be born again in His glory. May this book help you marvel anew at the message and meaning of that gift.

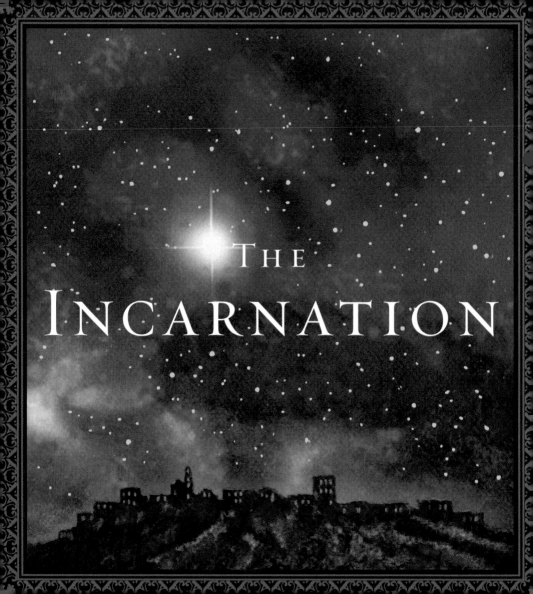

THE
INCARNATION

Christmas is not about the Savior's infancy; it is about His deity. The humble birth of Jesus Christ was never intended to be a façade to conceal the reality that God was being born into the world.

No one can really fathom what it means for God to be born in a manger. How does one explain the Almighty stooping to become a tiny infant? It was the greatest condescension the world has ever known or ever will know. Our minds cannot begin to understand what was in God's becoming a man. We will never comprehend why He who was infinitely rich would become poor, assume a human nature, and enter into a world He knew would reject Him and kill Him.

Nor can anyone explain how God could become a baby. Yet He did. Without forsaking His divine nature or diminishing His deity in any sense, He was born into our world as a tiny infant.

People often ask me if I think He cried, or if He needed the normal care and feeding one would give to any other baby. Of course He did. He was fully human with all the needs and emotions that are common to every human.

Yet He was also fully God—all wise and all powerful. How can both be true? I don't know. But the Bible clearly teaches that it is so. In some sense, Jesus voluntarily suspended the full application of His divine attributes. He didn't give up being God, but He willingly set aside the independent use of the privileges and powers that were His as God (Philippians 2:5–8). He chose to subjugate His will to His Father's will (John 5:30; 6:38). Through all that He remained fully God.

For nearly two thousand years, debate has been raging about who Jesus really is. Cults and skeptics have offered various explanations. They'll say He is one of many gods, a created being, a prophet, and so on. The common thread of all such theories is that they make Jesus less than God.

But let the Bible speak for itself. John's Gospel begins with a clear statement that Jesus is God: *"In the beginning was the Word, and the Word was with God, and the Word was God. He was in the beginning with God. All things came into being through Him, and apart from Him nothing came into being that has come into being."* Who is "the Word" spoken of in these verses? Verse 14 removes any doubt: *"And the Word became flesh, and dwelt among us, and we saw His glory, glory as of the only begotten from the Father, full of grace and truth."*

The biblical evidence is overwhelming that this child in the manger was the incarnation of God. For one thing, He was omniscient. John 2:24–25 says, *"But Jesus, on His part, was not entrusting Himself to them, for He knew all men, and because He did not need anyone to testify concerning man, for He Himself knew what was in man."* Nathanael was shocked to discover that Jesus knew all about him before they ever met, and it was enough to persuade him that Jesus was the Messiah (John 1:48–50). John 4 describes Jesus' meeting with a Samaritan woman at Jacob's well. He knew everything about her, too (vv. 17–19, 29).

Jesus also did the works of God, saying, *"Believe Me that I am in the Father and the Father is in Me; otherwise believe because of the works themselves"* (John 14:11). Jesus' works are convincing proof that He is God. He began His miraculous ministry with a simple act—He created wine at a wedding in Cana (John 2:1–11); only God can create. Moreover, He healed people who were hopelessly ill. He gave sight to the blind (Matthew 9:27–31). He opened ears that had never heard (Mark 7:31–37). He created enough fish and bread to feed thousands (Mark 6:48–52; 8:1–9). He raised the dead by simply commanding them to come forth from the grave (John 11:38–44).

THE FULLNESS OF GOD

There has never been another person like Jesus Christ. All the New Testament repeatedly stresses Jesus' deity. But let me point to one passage in particular, written by the apostle Paul, which captures the essence of Jesus' divine nature. These are the truths that make Christmas truly wonderful:

He is the image of the invisible God, the firstborn of all creation. For by Him all things were created, both in the heavens and on earth, visible and invisible, whether thrones or dominions or rulers or authorities—all things have been created through Him and for Him. He is before all things, and in Him all things hold together. He is also head of the body, the church; and He is the beginning, the firstborn from the dead, so that He Himself will come to have first place in everything. For it was the Father's good pleasure for all the fullness to dwell in Him, and through Him to reconcile all things to Himself, having made peace through the blood of His cross; through Him, I say, whether things on earth or things in heaven.

—COLOSSIANS 1:15–20

Through Christ, the invisible God has been made visible. God's full likeness is revealed in Jesus. And Jesus is not just an outline of God; He is fully God. Colossians 2:9 makes it even more explicit: *"For in Him all the fullness of Deity dwells in bodily form."* Nothing is lacking. No attribute is absent. He is God in the fullest possible sense, the perfect image.

Paul says Jesus is *"the firstborn of all creation"* (Colossians 1:15). Those who reject the deity of Christ have made much of that phrase, assuming it means Jesus was a created being. But the word translated "firstborn" is *prototokos*, which describes Jesus' rank, not His origin. The firstborn, the *prototokos*, in a Hebrew family was the heir, the ranking one, the one who had all the rights of inheritance. And in a royal family, the *prototokos* had the right to rule.

Christ is the One who inherits all creation and has the right to rule over it.

In Psalm 89:27, God says of David, *"I also shall make him My firstborn, the highest of the kings of the earth."* There the meaning of "firstborn" is given in plain language: *"the highest of the kings of the earth."* That's what *prototokos* means with regard to Christ—He is *"King of kings and Lord of lords"* (1 Timothy 6:15; Revelation 19:16). God has appointed His Son *"heir of all things"* (Hebrews 1:2). He is the primary One, the Son who has the right to the inheritance, the ranking Person, the Lord of all, heir of the whole of creation.

> HE WAS IN THE BEGINNING WITH GOD. ALL
> THINGS CAME INTO BEING THROUGH HIM, AND
> APART FROM HIM NOTHING CAME INTO BEING
> THAT HAS COME INTO BEING.
>
> *—John 1:2–3*

Christ is not only the heir of creation; He was also in the beginning the divine agent of creation, the Person of the Trinity through whom the world was made and for whom it was fashioned.

Think of what that means. The expanse of creation is staggering.

· A hollow ball the size of our sun would hold about one million planets the size of the earth.

· The brightest star in our sky, Sirius Canis Major, is twice as big as our sun.

· Arcturus is more than twenty-three times larger than our sun.

· Betelguese, one of the stars visible in the constellation Orion, is about three hundred times larger than our sun.

No wonder Job expressed his awe of God this way: *"How should man be just with God? . . . Which maketh Arcturus, Orion, and Pleiades, and the chambers of the south"* (Job 9:2, 9 KJV).

A ray of light travels about 186,000 miles per second. It takes eight–and–a–half minutes for light from the sun to reach us. If you could travel at that rate from earth, you could reach . . .

· the moon in a second and a half.

· Mars in four–and–a–half minutes.

· Jupiter in thirty–five minutes.

· Pluto in about five hours, twenty minutes.

· Alpha Centauri, the closest star, in four years, four months.

· Sirius in eight–and–a–half years.

· Arcturus in thirty–seven years.

· Betelgeuse in about 522 years.

If you could count the stars as you traveled across the Milky Way (a journey of about 100,000 years at light speed), you would find about one hundred billion stars, and there are billions more galaxies out there. The size of the universe is incomprehensible.

The baby in Bethlehem made all of it. He created everything.

> HE IS THE RADIANCE OF HIS GLORY AND THE EXACT REPRESENTATION OF HIS NATURE, AND UPHOLDS ALL THINGS BY THE WORD OF HIS POWER. WHEN HE HAD MADE PURIFICATION OF SINS, HE SAT DOWN AT THE RIGHT HAND OF THE MAJESTY ON HIGH.
> — *Hebrews 1:3*, emphasis added

Without Him, the whole world would fall apart. Don't buy the lie of deism, which says that God made everything, then wound it up like a clock, and went away. Far from deserting His creation, He stepped into it as a little infant with only a manger for His cradle.

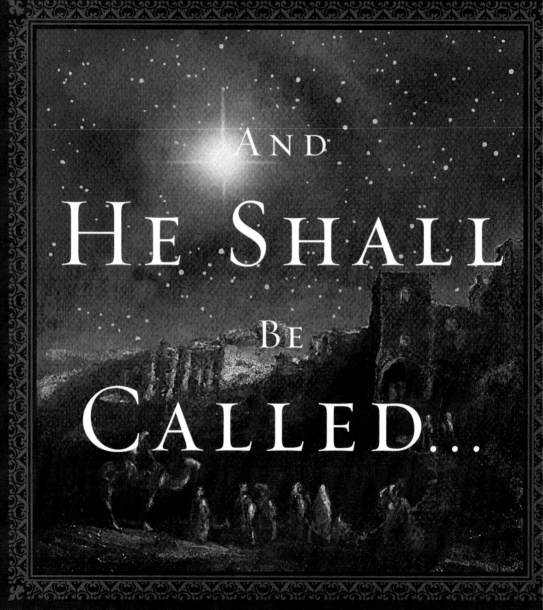

And He Shall Be Called...

"SHE WILL BEAR A SON; AND YOU SHALL CALL HIS
NAME JESUS, FOR HE WILL SAVE HIS PEOPLE
FROM THEIR SINS."

—*Matthew 1:21*

*G*od chose the name *Jesus* for His Son because its basic meaning defined the fundamental, overarching purpose for the Son's coming to earth. *Jesus* is the Greek form of the Hebrew *Joshua, Jeshua,* or *Jehoshua,* each of which means "Jehovah (Yaweh) will save." The baby Mary conceived by the power of the Holy Spirit and gave birth to in the plan of God would grow up to testify to the Father's salvation and would Himself be that salvation. By His own sacrificial death on the cross and triumphant resurrection from the grave He would save His own—all those who are drawn from sin to repentance and who receive faith to embrace His atoning work.

"BEHOLD, THE VIRGIN SHALL BE WITH CHILD AND SHALL BEAR A SON, AND THEY SHALL CALL HIS NAME IMMANUEL," WHICH TRANSLATED MEANS, "GOD WITH US."

—*Matthew 1:23*

The name *Immanuel* is the heart of the Christmas story. It is a Hebrew name that means, literally, "God with us." It is a promise of incarnate deity, a promise that God Himself would appear as a human infant, Immanuel, "God with us." This baby who was to be born would be God Himself in human form.

If we could condense all the truths of Christmas into only three words, these would be the words: "God with us." We tend to focus our attention at Christmas on the *infancy* of Christ, but the greater truth of the holiday is His *deity*. More astonishing than a baby in the manger is the truth that this promised baby is the omnipotent Creator of the heavens and the earth!

Immanuel, infinitely rich, became poor. He assumed our nature, entered our sin–polluted world, took our guilt on Himself although He was sinless, bore our griefs, carried our sorrows, was wounded for our transgressions, bruised for our iniquities (Isaiah 53:5). All of that is wrapped up in "God with us."

The apostle Paul penned one of the gladdest truths in all of Scripture: *"For you know the grace of our Lord Jesus Christ, that though He was rich, yet for your sake He became poor, so that you through His poverty might become rich"* (2 Corinthians 8:9). That's the immeasurable gift of Christmas. Christ, God's own Son, gave up His wealth and privilege to live as God with us, that He might save His people from their sins, and that through His poverty might become rich.

"FOR TODAY IN THE CITY OF DAVID THERE HAS BEEN
BORN FOR YOU A SAVIOR, WHO IS CHRIST THE LORD."
—*Luke 2:11*

Christ is an exalted title for a baby born in a humble stable. Jesus wore no crown and had no halo over His head to identify Him as someone special. There were no outward marks of His deity, sovereignty, or Messiahship. But when the angel announced Jesus' birth to the shepherds, he identified the One born that night by His twofold heavenly title, "Christ the Lord."

In both the Greek translation of the Old Testament and in the Greek New Testament, the title *Christos* ("Christ") means "the anointed one." That usage in reference to the future Savior occurs as early as Daniel 9:25–26 (where *Christos* is simply the equivalent of the Hebrew *Messiah*). Whenever the term was used in biblical times, it signified that an ultimate authority was anointing someone and placing him in a very high office. In Jesus' case, the ultimate authority who anointed Him was His Father. God declared that Jesus is the King. He is the eternal King of kings who will sit on David's throne and reign over His Kingdom forever. Jesus, at the very end of His earthly ministry, confirmed the truth of His Kingship in this exchange

with Pontius Pilate: *"Pilate therefore said to Him, 'Are You a king, then?' Jesus answered, 'You say rightly that I am a king. For this cause I was born, and for this cause I have come into the world, that I should bear witness to the truth'"* (John 18:37 NKJV).

When the angel called Jesus "Christ the Lord," he was not using a mere human designation of *lord*. Instead, he was using a divine designation and claiming that the Child in Bethlehem is God. To say that Jesus is Lord is to say that He is first and foremost God. This is the most fundamental and essential confession of the Christian faith. It is unequivocal that if any person desires to be saved, he must make the heartfelt and vocal confession that Jesus is Lord (Romans 10:9). In addition, the expression "Jesus is Lord" implies all the sovereignty and authority associated with One who is God. For "Lord" in Luke 2:11, the angel used the Greek word *kurios*, which expresses an authority that is valid and lawful. The ultimate lawful authority in the universe is God, and the angel was declaring Jesus' lawful authority as the Son of God. The Greek translators of the Old Testament and the writers of the New Testament used *kurios* so often to refer to God that the word became synonymous for the name of God. When the angel declared Jesus to be Lord, he was declaring Him to be the true God, the One who possesses all authority and sovereignty.

CHILD OF PROPHECY.

The Christmas story in the Bible begins several hundred years before that night in Bethlehem. One Old Testament prophecy after another promised a coming savior—the Messiah, the Anointed One— who would redeem the people of God. The centerpiece of all the Christmas prophecies, Isaiah 9:6, was written nearly six hundred years before Jesus' birth. Isaiah promised it would be a miraculous event, unlike any the world had ever known, and the details Isaiah gave were fulfilled precisely by Jesus.

> FOR A CHILD WILL BE BORN TO US, A SON WILL BE GIVEN TO US; AND THE GOVERNMENT WILL REST ON HIS SHOULDERS; AND HIS NAME WILL BE CALLED WONDERFUL COUNSELOR, MIGHTY GOD, ETERNAL FATHER, PRINCE OF PEACE.
>
> —*Isaiah 9:6*

Isaiah 9:6 is the most familiar of all the Old Testament prophecies about the birth of Christ. Handel included it as one of the great choruses of his *Messiah* oratorio. Chances are you either sing it or hear it several times every Christmas season. Consider the rich truth in this one short verse and the attributes given to this extraordinary child. To the Jewish nation, Isaiah's prophecy was news of a coming King. To the unsuspecting world, the prophecy promised a Savior, God incarnate, whose coming would dramatically and forever alter human history.

SON OF MAN. *"A child will be born to us"* is a statement about His humanity. He began life like any other human—as an infant. Isaiah doesn't say more about this here, but we know from the New Testament that Christ experienced every temptation common to humanity, but He never sinned (Hebrews 4:15). As a man, He felt everything we feel, hurt like we hurt, wept like we weep, and in His death He even felt the weight of sin as He took ours upon Himself.

SON OF GOD. *"A son will be given to us"* speaks of the Savior's preexistent diety. By saying "given," not "born," Isaiah suggests that Jesus existed before His birth. He was already God, the second Person of the Trinity, before He was given to us to be our Savior (Philippians 2:6–7). He came as the Son of God— God in a human body—to conquer sin and death forever. He is the perfect Son of God, the promise of the ages, the Holy One of Israel, the desire of nations, the light in darkness, the only hope for our lost world.

KING OF KINGS. *"The government will rest on His shoulders"* looks beyond that first Christmas to a time still in the prophetic future when Christ shall reign over a literal, earthly, geopolitical kingdom that encompasses all the kingdoms and governments of the world (Zechariah 14:9; Daniel 2:44). In that day, the government of the whole world will rest on His shoulders, and He will reign as sovereign over a worldwide kingdom of righteousness and peace. In the meantime, His government operates in secret. His kingdom and sovereign rule are manifest within those who trust Him as their Lord (Luke 17:20–21).

WONDERFUL COUNSELOR. Messiah's kingdom has the answer to the world's confusion. During His incarnation, Christ demonstrated His wisdom as a counselor. When people came to Him, He always knew what to say, when to reach out to a seeking heart, and when to rebuke an impetuous soul. The testimony of those who heard Him was, *"Never has a man spoken the way this man speaks"* (John 7:46). Christ is the source of all truth (John 14:6), and it is to Him that we must turn to make sense of life's confusion. Jesus is the Counselor who knows everything. He knows all about you; He knows the needs of your heart; He knows how to answer those needs. And He always gives wise counsel to those who will hear and obey Him.

MIGHTY GOD.   The King is the Mighty God and His kingdom is free from all chaos. *"God is not a God of confusion but of peace"* (1 Corinthians 14:33), which means chaos is antithetical to who He is. Christ the King loves to step into a life of chaos and not only provide wonderful counsel, but also display His divine power by bringing order. He not only tells His subjects what to do as a Wonderful Counselor, but He can energize them to do it—because He is the Mighty God. In Jesus we have a sovereign Master who can forgive sin, defeat Satan, liberate us from the power of evil, redeem us, answer our prayers, restore our broken souls, and reign over rebuilt lives, bringing order to chaos.

ETERNAL FATHER. We tend to cringe at the word "government," picturing an administrative labyrinth, but our Messiah's kingdom is not like that. He requires no bureaucracy; He shoulders His government by Himself. He can do it because He is the eternal Father, or as the phrase in Isaiah 9:6 is literally translated, "the Father of Eternity." Christ is Creator of heaven and earth. According to God the Father's own testimony, the Son—Jesus—was the Person of the Godhead who created time out of eternity and fashioned the universe from nothing (Hebrews 1:10–12). Nothing is too difficult for the Creator and Sustainer of everything. Infinity and all its intricacies are nothing to Him who is the Alpha and Omega, the First and Last, the Beginning and the End—the Father of Eternity. He declares the end from the beginning (Isaiah 46:10). He is in complete and sovereign control, He sees the end of everything, and He guarantees that all things will work together for the ultimate good of all His kingdom's subjects (Romans 8:28).

PRINCE OF PEACE. In Messiah's kingdom there are no conflicts because He is the Prince of Peace. He offers *peace from God* (Romans 1:7) to all who receive His grace. He makes *peace with God* (Romans 5:1) for those who surrender to Him in faith. And He brings the *peace of God* (Philippians 4:7) to those who walk with Him. As we hear so often at Christmas, the beginning of His earthly life was heralded by angels who pronounced peace on earth (Luke 2:14). There never really has been peace on earth in the sense we think of it. Wars and rumors of wars have characterized the entire two millennia since that first Christmas, as well as all the time before it. The announcement of peace on earth was a two-pronged proclamation. First, it declared the arrival of the only One who ultimately can bring lasting peace on earth (which He will do when He returns to bring about the final establishment of His earthly kingdom). But more importantly, it was a proclamation that God's peace is available to men and women. Read the words of Luke 2:14 carefully and note this emphasis: *"Glory to God in the highest, and on earth peace among men with* WHOM HE IS PLEASED." God is pleased with the people who yield their lives to Him. *"The* LORD *takes pleasure in those who fear Him, in those who hope in His mercy"* (Psalm 147:11 NKJV). When the angels proclaimed peace on earth, they were speaking primarily of a very personal, individual application of God's peace that grows out of a firsthand knowledge of the Prince of Peace.

Isaiah 9:7 elaborates on the peace that Christ's kingdom will bring on earth:

> There will be no end to the increase of
>   His government or of peace,
> On the throne of David and over his kingdom,
> To establish it and to uphold it with justice
>   and righteousness
> From then on and forevermore
> The zeal of the LORD of hosts will
>   accomplish this.

In other words, His perfect government and perfect peace will keep expanding, getting better and better. How can anything perfect get better? That's one of the mysteries of Messiah's reign. It just gets better and better, and the perfect peace gets deeper and deeper.

The prophetic message of Christmas is the good news of God's answer to all the confusion, chaos, complexities, and conflicts of life. It is the gift of the newborn infant who is also the Father of all eternity. He is an innocent child, yet He is a wise Counselor and mighty King. He is God with us. *Immanuel*.

Let Him be God with *you*.

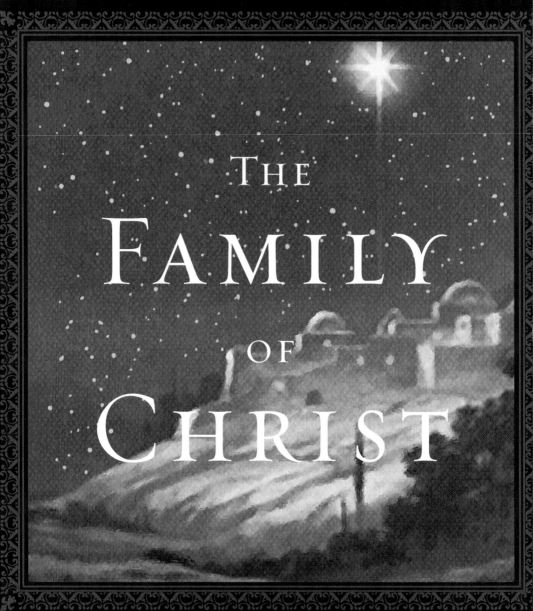

THE
FAMILY
OF
CHRIST

istory has romanticized Joseph and Mary. We tend to think of them as larger than life. Artists often picture them with mystic expressions and halos around their heads. In reality they were common folk. Joseph was a carpenter, and Mary was a young girl from a simple background. They could hardly have been plainer. Only their faith was extraordinary.

In all likelihood, Joseph and Mary were young, probably in their teens, because marriages in their culture tended to be arranged at a young age. Betrothals often occurred when girls were as young as twelve or thirteen. What we do know about Mary indicates she had reached a level of maturity beyond most teenagers, so perhaps she was in her late teens. Joseph was probably not much older.

Their lives were forever changed when the archangel Gabriel appeared to Mary with the announcement that she would bear a son. Mary's faith is a wonderful example for us. Rather than resentfully looking at her pregnancy as unfair and embarrassing, she understood that she had been uniquely blessed by God (Luke 1:48–49). Joseph, too, is a remarkable example of extraordinary faith. Understandably distressed when he discovered Mary was going to have a baby, he nevertheless accepted the difficult consequences of God's will for their lives. Though they must have suffered tremendously from the lies and innuendo of cruel gossipmongers, Joseph and Mary were steadfast. They probably didn't understand the fullness of God's plan, but they followed unwaveringly. They were ideal earthly parents for God's only begotten Son.

BORN OF A VIRGIN

Now the birth of Jesus Christ was as follows: when His mother Mary had been betrothed to Joseph, before they came together she was found to be with child by the Holy Spirit. And Joseph her husband, being a righteous man and not wanting to disgrace her, planned to send her away secretly. But when he had considered this, behold, an angel of the Lord appeared to him in a dream, saying, "Joseph, son of David, do not be afraid to take Mary as your wife; for the Child who has been conceived in her is of the Holy Spirit. She will bear a Son; and you shall call His name Jesus, for He will save His people from their sins." Now all this took place to fulfill what was spoken by the Lord through the prophet: "BEHOLD, THE VIRGIN SHALL BE WITH CHILD AND SHALL BEAR A SON, AND THEY SHALL CALL HIS NAME IMMANUEL," which translated means, "GOD WITH US." And Joseph awoke from his sleep and did as the angel of the Lord commanded him, and took Mary as his wife, but kept her a virgin until she gave birth to a Son; and he called His name Jesus.

— MATTHEW 1:18–25

No other fact in the Christmas story is more important than the virgin birth. The virgin birth must have happened exactly the way Scripture says. Otherwise, Christmas has no point at all. If Jesus is simply the illegitimate child of Mary's infidelity, or even if He is the child of Joseph's marital union with Mary, then He is not God. If He is not God, His claims are lies. If His claims are lies, His salvation is a hoax. And if His salvation is a hoax, we are all doomed.

The virgin birth is an underlying assumption in everything the Bible says about Jesus. To reject the virgin birth is to reject Christ's deity, the accuracy and authority of Scripture, and a host of other related doctrines at the heart of the Christian faith. No issue is more important than the virgin birth to our understanding of who Jesus is. If we deny that Jesus is God, we have denied the very essence of Christianity. Everything else the Bible teaches about Christ hinges on the truth we celebrate at Christmas—that Jesus is God in human flesh. If the story of His birth is merely a fabrication or trumped–up legend, then so is what the rest of Scripture tells about Him. The virgin birth is as crucial as the resurrection in substantiating His deity. It is not an optional truth. Anyone who rejects Christ's deity rejects Christ absolutely (1 John 4:1–3).

Jesus Himself viewed the question of His parentage as a watershed issue, and it was a hot topic in several run–ins with the Pharisees. One of the best–known confrontations happened the week before the crucifixion.

> *While the Pharisees were gathered together, Jesus asked them a question: "What do you think about the Christ, whose son is He?" They said to Him, "The son of David." He said to them, "Then how does David in the Spirit call Him 'Lord,' saying,*
>
> > *'THE LORD SAID TO MY LORD,*
> > *"SIT AT MY RIGHT HAND,*
> > *UNTIL I PUT YOUR ENEMIES*
> > *BENEATH YOUR FEET"'?*
>
> *"If David then calls Him 'Lord,' how is He his son?"*
>
> *No one was able to answer Him a word, nor did anyone dare from that day on to ask Him another question.*
>
> —MATTHEW 22:41–46

On another occasion, the Pharisees told Jesus, "*We were not born of fornication; we have one Father: God*" (John 8:41). They were implying that Jesus was born illegitimately. They twisted the whole point of His miraculous birth to call Him a bastard child.

There is a direct parallel between those ancient Pharisees and today's religious leaders who hint that the virgin birth is unimportant or a fable. Their challenges grow out of unbelief in Jesus Christ. They are an expression of sinful, unregenerate hearts. Contrast their response to Jesus' sonship with that of Peter's declaration in Matthew 16:13–17:

> *Now when Jesus came into the district of Caesarea Philippi, He was asking His disciples, "Who do people say that the Son of Man is?"*
>
> *And they said, "Some say John the Baptist; and others, Elijah; but still others, Jeremiah, or one of the prophets."*
>
> *He said to them, "But who do you say that I am?"*
>
> *Simon Peter answered, "You are the Christ, the Son of the living God."*

And Jesus said to him, "Blessed are you, Simon Barjona, because flesh and blood did not reveal this to you, but My Father who is in heaven."

Peter understood that Jesus was more than a human messiah, more than an anointed prophet, more than a son of David. He was the Son of the living God. Peter knew this because God revealed it to him. Flesh and blood cannot reach that conclusion. Science, philosophy, and human religion cannot explain who Jesus is. Their adherents will inevitably conclude that He is a great teacher, a good moral example, or even a prophet of God. But they all miss the fact that He is the Son of the living God.

That's why the virgin birth is so important. For Jesus to be God, He must be born of God. Joseph (a man) and Mary (a woman) cannot produce God. God cannot be born into this world by natural human processes. There's no way He could be God apart from being conceived by God.

As far back as the earliest chapters in Genesis, we find hints that God would send a virgin-born redeemer. After Adam and Eve disobeyed God and ate the forbidden fruit, God pronounced this curse on the serpent, Satan: *"I will put enmity between you and the woman, and between your seed and her seed; he shall bruise you on the head, and you shall bruise him on the heel"* (Genesis 3:15). "Her seed" is an expression used nowhere else in Scripture. Everywhere else when Scripture speaks of someone's offspring as "seed," it is speaking of the male seed, or sperm. Only one time does Scripture ever speak of the seed of a woman, and that's an indication of something special. God said Satan would war against the woman's seed, and we know the fulfillment of that prophecy: Satan "bruised" Christ on the cross, but our Lord's death and resurrection ultimately turned out to be a crushing blow to the head of Satan.

Isaiah 7:14 also prophesies the virgin birth: *"Therefore the Lord Himself will give you a sign: Behold, a virgin will be with child and bear a son, and she will call His name Immanuel."* Those who reject the Messianic intent of this verse point out that the Hebrew word translated "virgin" here—*almah*—can also mean "young girl." But *almah* appears only nine times in the Old Testament, and eight of those nine times the word must mean "virgin." Also, if this is just any young woman having a baby, that's no sign; lots of young women have babies. A sign is meant to get your attention. When God gave this sign, He was pointing to something extraordinary, and a virgin bearing a son would indeed be a sign. Matthew 1:23 was originally written in Greek, while Isaiah 7:14 was originally written in Hebrew. When Matthew wrote the divine interpretation to Isaiah's prophecy, he translated the Hebrew word *almah* as *parthenos*, which can't mean anything but "virgin," one who has known only sexual abstinence.

Mary and Joseph faithfully abstained from sexual relations with one another during the engagement period, as their marriage contract required. That was also in accord with God's high regard for sexual purity and His commands for sexual abstinence prior to the marriage ceremony and for sexual fidelity afterward. Thus, Mary's virginity was an important indicator of her godliness.

The amazing fact of Jesus' supernatural birth is the only way to explain the perfect, sinless life He lived while on earth. A skeptic once asked a Christian, "If I told you that boy over there was born without a human father, would you believe me?" "Yes," the believer replied, "if he lived as Jesus lived."

Thus began the Christmas story. Quietly, without public fanfare, God's Son was conceived in a young woman who had never known intimacy with any man. The chain of events this set off would change Mary's life—and Joseph's—forever. More than that, the Son from on high would alter the course of all human history. Clearly, Jesus was God's own Son.

Extraordinary births occurred throughout biblical history. For example:

· As God promised, Isaac was born to Abraham and Sarah in their old age (Genesis 17:19–22; 21:1–3).

· As God promised, Samson was born to Manoah and his barren wife (Judges 13).

· In answer to the prayer of a godly mother, Samuel was born to Hannah and Elkanah (1 Samuel 1).

· When the time came for the forerunner of Christ to be born, God blessed Elizabeth and Zacharias with John the Baptist (Luke 1:15–17, 76–79).

But none of those special births was as amazing as the virgin birth of the Son of God, our Lord and Savior Jesus Christ.

MARY

Luke 1:27 says Mary was engaged to Joseph. Engagement in that culture did not mean the same thing it means today. The rabbinical writings distinguish two stages in Hebrew marriage. The *kiddushin*, or betrothal period, was legally as binding as marriage. If at any time during the *kiddushin* either of the couple violated the vows or was found to be unchaste, a formal divorce was required to nullify the marriage contract. In other words, the man and woman were legally married—and were even called husband and wife—but they still lived in separate homes and had no physical relationship whatsoever. The second stage of Hebrew marriage, the *huppa*, was like a modern wedding, only a much bigger occasion. Weddings often lasted seven days. It was such a wedding in Cana where Jesus worked His first public miracle by turning water into wine (John 2:1–11). If the ceremony had been going on for seven days, it's little wonder that they ran short of wine!

Mary's pregnancy began during their *kiddushin*. She and Joseph had entered into a marriage contract but were still living separately when, nine months before that first Christmas, the archangel appeared to Mary.

> Now in the sixth month the angel Gabriel was sent from God to a city in Galilee called Nazareth, to a virgin engaged to a man whose name was Joseph, of the descendants of David; and the virgin's name was Mary. And coming in, he said to her, "Greetings, favored one! The Lord is with you." But she was very perplexed at this statement, and kept pondering what kind of salutation this was.

> The angel said to her, "Do not be afraid, Mary; for you have found favor with God. And behold, you will conceive in your womb and bear a son, and you shall name Him Jesus. He will be great and will be called the Son of the Most High; and the Lord God will give Him the throne of His father David; and He will reign over the house of Jacob forever, and His kingdom will have no end."

> Mary said to the angel, "How can this be, since I am a virgin?"

> The angel answered and said to her, "The Holy Spirit will come upon you, and the power of the Most High will overshadow you; and for that reason the holy Child shall be

called the Son of God. And behold, even your relative Elizabeth has also conceived a son in her old age; and she who was called barren is now in her sixth month. For nothing will be impossible with God."

And Mary said, "Behold, the bondslave of the Lord; may it be done to me according to your word." And the angel departed from her.

—LUKE 1:26–38

This is the angel's promise that God was coming into the world, but it's not the first time God made such a promise. Gabriel's announcement actually heralded the beginning of the promise's fulfillment. The monumental news of the Incarnation broke with supernatural surprise to Mary. The news was part of God's plan of redemption, which He devised even before creating the world. God originally established the hope of a Savior in Genesis 3:15, and the inspired authors of the Old Testament kept it alive for millennia in the hearts of believers (Genesis 49:10; Deuteronomy 18:15; Psalm 2:6–12; Isaiah 7:14; 9:6–7; 52:13–53:12; Daniel 2:45; 7:13–14; 9:26; Micah 5:2). In fact, the

Old Testament contains about 350 prophecies and promises concerning the coming Messiah.

A supernatural, miraculous tone permeates that entire account. The angel, the Holy Spirit, the prophetic utterance, the Son of God conceived by a miracle in Mary's womb, Elizabeth's pregnancy despite the fact that she was old and formerly barren—all those elements add to the sense that something dramatic and miraculous was taking place.

We don't know much else about Mary's background from Scripture. By comparing the gospel records, we discover that she had a sister named Salome, the mother of Zebedee's children (Matthew 27:56; Mark 15:40; John 19:25). Zebedee was the father of the apostles James and John. They were all simple fishermen (Matthew 4:21–22). Luke says Elizabeth, mother of John the Baptist, was a relative of Mary (Luke 1:36). Luke's genealogy refers to Mary's father as Eli (3:23). Other than that, we know almost nothing about Mary. Her early life was spent in Nazareth. She was probably from a poor family and was no doubt a hardworking, exceptionally virtuous, and godly young woman.

The simplicity of Mary's faith is remarkable, given the circumstances. Her simple answer, *"Behold, the bondslave of the Lord; may it be done to me according to your word"* (Luke 1:38), gives us insight into her character. Quietly, modestly, she saw her role as a simple servant of the Lord. She might have been tempted to either boast or rebel, but she did neither. Luke 2:19 further reveals Mary's godly character, showing her typical response to the extraordinary work of God in her life: *"Mary treasured all these things, pondering them in her heart."* (See also 2:51.)

It's hard to imagine a more gracious response to the angel's announcement than Mary's. Certainly her response shows deep and mature faith. Mary simply submitted to God's plan for her. Luke 1:46–55 records her response, known as the Magnificat:

> *And Mary said: "My soul exalts the Lord, and my spirit has rejoiced in God my Savior. For He has had regard for the humble state of His bondslave; for behold, from this time on all generations will count me blessed. For the Mighty One has done great things for me; and holy is His name. AND HIS MERCY IS UPON GENERATION AFTER*

GENERATION TOWARD THOSE WHO FEAR HIM. He has done mighty deeds with His arm; He has scattered those who were proud in the thoughts of their heart. He has brought down rulers from their thrones, and has exalted those who were humble. HE HAS FILLED THE HUNGRY WITH GOOD THINGS; and sent away the rich empty—handed. He has given help to Israel His servant, in remembrance of His mercy, as He spoke to our fathers, to Abraham and his descendants forever."

These words reveal a singular faith. There was no questioning in her mind, no doubt, no misgivings, no fear, no demanding to understand—only an instant submission and the confidence that this was God's truth. She expressed her heart in praise.

When you think about it, God's sovereign choice of Mary to be the mother of Jesus is astonishing. Out of all the women He could have chosen—queens, princesses, or daughters of the wealthy and influential—He chose an unknown, unassuming young woman from an obscure village. But God's plans and purposes often do not unfold in the manner we, as humans, would have selected.

As good and godly as she was, Mary was still a sinner in need of God's grace, just like you and me, and God freely gave her His favor and blessing (Luke 1:28, 30). She knew she didn't deserve God's grace, so she praised Him and called Him *"God my Savior"* (Luke 1:47). Mary knew what all righteous, believing people know—that she needed a Savior. And that is probably the best indication we have that Mary was a true believer. All genuinely righteous people are distressed when they face God (or in Mary's case, one of His holy angels), because they know they're sinners. As she pondered Gabriel's message, Mary might've asked herself over and over, *Why would God choose me, an unworthy sinner, to be the recipient of His amazing grace? Why would the Lord single me out for such special privilege?* Nothing on earth could have prepared her for such a breathtaking announcement, not to mention the fear that usually accompanies a visit from an angel. Therefore, it was appropriate that the angel would give Mary some words of assurance: *"The angel said to her, 'Do not be afraid, Mary; for you have found favor with God'"* (Luke 1:30). So why did God choose Mary? Not because she was perfect, but because it suited His good pleasure and perfect plan. The issue was not Mary's individual worthiness or human merit, it was God's sovereign choice. God's special blessing to Mary boldly highlights the truth that the Lord grants abundant grace to His chosen ones.

GREAT IS THE MYSTERY OF GODLINESS:
GOD WAS MANIFESTED IN THE FLESH,
JUSTIFIED IN THE SPIRIT,
SEEN BY ANGELS,
PREACHED AMONG THE GENTILES,
BELIEVED ON IN THE WORLD,
RECEIVED UP IN GLORY.

—1 Timothy 3:16 NKJV

MARY & ELIZABETH

L uke begins his Gospel with the story of two conception miracles, both involving women who could not naturally have children. Elizabeth was in her sixties or seventies, barren, and yet with her elderly husband, Zacharias, she conceived and carried in her womb John the Baptist, the prophesied forerunner of the Messiah (Isaiah 40:3; Malachi 3:1). Mary was a young virgin who became pregnant by the power of the Holy Spirit and as a result would give birth to Jesus, the incarnate Son of God.

Even though there were differences in their ages and circumstances, both Elizabeth and Mary were women chosen by God to be human instruments in the two most unusual and significant births in the New Testament. The births marked the great peak in redemptive history, and the Holy Spirit providentially filled the two accounts with incredible, unmistakable similarities:

· Both accounts begin with an introduction of the child's parents, or parent.

· Both mention specific obstacles to childbearing—Elizabeth's barrenness and Mary's virginity.

· The angel Gabriel made both announcements.

· Both women lived in small towns. Elizabeth and Zacharias lived in the hill country south of Jerusalem; Mary lived in Nazareth, a small Galilean town north of Jerusalem.

· In both stories there was a fearful reaction to Gabriel's words and a statement of reassurance from him.

· Both accounts included a description of the coming son.

· Both times there was raised an objection from the one hearing the angel's news; Zacharias voiced unbelief, and Mary expressed lack of understanding.

· Before Gabriel's respective departures, he guaranteed his announcement would come to pass.

It's easy to deduce why Mary would have wanted to meet with Elizabeth as soon as possible. The news Mary had just heard from Gabriel was startling, even scary. The angel understood how Mary was feeling and graciously told her of God's sign that prompted her to journey eighty miles to Elizabeth's home: *"And behold, even your relative Elizabeth has also conceived a son in her old age; and she who was called barren is now in her sixth month. For nothing will be impossible with God.'"* (Luke 1:36–37).

Mary believed the angel, but it's easy to understand that Mary would welcome anything that might bolster her faith—anything that might underscore the reality that such miracles do occur. After all, the conception that would take place within her body would be completely the result of God's miraculous intervention without her even knowing exactly when it happened. Those unique circumstances lead inevitably to further questions. How could Mary withstand the emotional and spiritual strain that went with being the mother of God's Son? And because her pregnancy would not be physically noticeable for a period of time, how could Mary be certain right away that the angel's words had really come to pass? All of those factors compelled Mary to go without delay to visit Elizabeth—the one person who could verify for her that God was able to perform a conception miracle.

The Lord arranged for Mary and Elizabeth's meeting as a sign of the truth of Gabriel's words to Mary. The two cousins definitely had a lot to talk about. Just listening to Elizabeth and realizing she was indeed pregnant provided a great personal confirmation to Mary. Because God fulfilled what He had promised to Elizabeth, surely he would also fulfill what He had promised to Mary. Elizabeth was the one person who would really understand and believe Mary's story, because Elizabeth was a living testimony that God was doing conception miracles. What a tremendous affirmation that must have been for Mary!

During her visit with Elizabeth, Mary also witnessed an amazing physical phenomenon that further confirmed for her that God had placed within her body His only begotten Son. *"When Elizabeth heard Mary's greeting, the baby leaped in her womb"* (Luke 1:41). This movement of Elizabeth's baby was far more significant than the normal kicking of a baby in the womb. The special leap of this baby was the first proclamation of the greatest prophet who ever lived—John the Baptist, the forerunner announcing Christ's coming. The unborn John was also fulfilling part of the angel's prophecy to his father, Zacharias: *"'He will be filled with the Holy Spirit while yet in his mother's womb'"* (Luke 1:15). The divinely inspired delight John displayed foreshadowed his teaching later: "'He who has the bride is the bridegroom; but the friend of the bridegroom, who stands and hears him, rejoices greatly because of the bridegroom's voice. So this joy of mine has been made full'" (John 3:29).

> Now Mary arose in those days and went into the hill country with haste, to a city of Judah, and entered the house of Zacharias and greeted Elizabeth. And it happened, when Elizabeth heard the greeting of Mary, that the babe leaped in her womb; and Elizabeth was filled with the Holy Spirit. Then she spoke out with a loud voice and said, "Blessed are you among women, and blessed is the fruit of your womb! But why is this granted to me, that the mother of my Lord should come to me? For indeed, as soon as the voice of your greeting sounded in my ears, the babe leaped in my womb for joy. Blessed is she who believed, for there will be a fulfillment of those things which were told her from the Lord."
>
> —LUKE 1:39–45 NKJV

During Mary's visit with Elizabeth, Mary received another confirmation that the angel's recent announcement was true when Elizabeth was inspired by the Holy Spirit. Being filled with the Holy Spirit was often linked to speaking a message from God (2 Samuel 23:2; Luke 1:67; 2:25–28; 2 Peter 1:21), and the Spirit filled Elizabeth with enthusiasm over the incredible truth that Mary was going to bear the Christ. Elizabeth's message pronounced several blessings.

BLESSING ON MARY. *"Blessed are you among women."* This sweeping statement is from a Hebrew phrase that means, "You're the most blessed of all women." In ancient Jewish culture, a woman's greatness was based on the greatness of the children she bore (Luke 11:27), and Elizabeth was telling Mary that she was most blessed because she was going to give birth to the greatest child ever, the Lord Jesus.

BLESSING FOR THE CHILD. *"Blessed is the fruit of your womb!"* Elizabeth knew Mary's baby would receive the full, unmitigated blessing of heaven. He would be holy, blameless, and perfectly sinless. He would receive all that the Father possesses, including a vast body of redeemed men and women to serve, praise, and glorify Him forever.

BLESSING OF HERSELF. In amazement, humility, and joy Elizabeth wondered aloud how and why the mother of her Lord would visit her. In this prophetic confirmation, Elizabeth acknowledged that the unborn Jesus was already the Lord.

BLESSING ON ALL WHO BELIEVE. *"Blessed is she who believed that there would be a fulfillment of what had been spoken to her from the Lord.'"* Certainly, Elizabeth directed this beatitude toward Mary, but its being in the third person demonstrates that the Spirit widened this blessing to include anyone who believes God's revelation.

Mary is a model of faith. She believed that the angel's divine message to her would be fulfilled. And she settled that faith in her heart and mind by pursuing a sure confirmation of the truth from Elizabeth. After Mary received Elizabeth's confirmation and encouragement, she must have rejoiced as she returned home three months later to face her fiancé, Joseph, with news of her miraculous pregnancy.

JOSEPH

Initial news of Mary's pregnancy presented Joseph with a twofold problem. First, as a caring and responsible person concerned about doing the right thing, Joseph was unwilling to proceed with his original plans (wedding Mary) once he perceived that a crucial part of those plans was no longer acceptable (Mary's pregnancy). His difficulty was intensified by the reality that he was a righteous man, genuinely concerned about doing what was morally and ethically right according to God's Law. Joseph's second difficult decision concerned how he should then treat Mary. We don't know if he felt anger, resentment, or bitterness, but he certainly experienced shame at what he had to assume was true: that Mary had been unfaithful to him. However, Joseph's concern was not primarily with his own shame and embarrassment, but with Mary's (Matthew 1:19).

We know nothing about Joseph's background either. He is called a "carpenter" (Matthew 13:55). The Greek word also can be translated "woodworker" or "mason." It may have been that he did both. If he built houses he would need to be able to lay bricks and frame windows and doors, too. At any rate, he worked hard for a living and probably was anything but rich.

He was a godly man of faith, however. Matthew 1:19 calls him "a righteous man." Matthew tells the story from Joseph's point of view:

> Now the birth of Jesus Christ was as follows: when His mother Mary had been betrothed to Joseph, before they came together she was found to be with child by the Holy Spirit. And Joseph her husband, being a righteous man and not wanting to disgrace her, planned to send her away secretly. But when he had considered this, behold, an angel of the Lord appeared to him in a dream, saying, "Joseph, son of David, do not be afraid to take Mary as your wife; for the Child who has been conceived in her is of the Holy Spirit. She will bear a Son; and you shall call His name Jesus, for He will save His people from their sins." Now all this took place to fulfill what was spoken by the Lord through the prophet: "BEHOLD, THE VIRGIN SHALL BE WITH CHILD AND SHALL BEAR A SON, AND THEY SHALL CALL HIS NAME IMMANUEL," which

translated means, "GOD WITH US." And Joseph awoke from his sleep and did as the angel of the Lord commanded him, and took Mary as his wife, but kept her a virgin until she gave birth to a Son; and he called His name Jesus.

—MATTHEW 1:18–25

Joseph, a just and righteous man, was deeply committed to Mary. No doubt he was looking forward to the day when they could come together as man and wife. He was jolted by the news that Mary was pregnant. He knew the quality of her character. He knew the righteous standard by which she lived. He knew her commitment to God. He knew a premarital pregnancy was totally out of character. It made no sense at all. Joseph must have felt his whole world was coming to an end.

The law of Israel demanded that a woman who became pregnant outside of marriage should be put to death (Deuteronomy 22:20–21). In fact, the penalty for almost every sexual sin was death. Had they been living in Moses' day, Mary would have been immediately stoned. But the laxness of the Jewish theocracy and the infiltration of Roman law in Joseph's day gave him two other options. One, he could make her a public example. That is, he could charge her with adultery in a public court. She would be shamed, brought to trial, convicted in front of everyone, and forever ruined in terms of reputation. The other possibility was that he could quietly write a bill of divorce before two or three witnesses and end their relationship. There would be no fanfare. Nobody would need to know. She could simply go away somewhere and secretly bear and raise the child.

Joseph loved Mary. He didn't want to make her a public example, but he couldn't marry her if she was guilty of harlotry. He decided to divorce or put her away privately. He must have spent considerable time considering his options, because before he had time to act—Scripture says, *"While he thought on these things"* (Matthew 1:20 KJV)—the Lord intervened. Joseph was meditating, mulling over what he had to do. And while he was still pondering his options, he fell asleep and received the dream from God.

Mary had no way to protect her reputation. She could have tried explaining to Joseph that the baby was conceived by God, but do you think he would have instantly believed her? In all of human history there had never been a virgin birth. So the Spirit of God became her advocate. The Lord, in His sovereign providence and wonderful grace, sent an angel who appeared to Joseph in a dream and dispelled the cloud of suspicion and shame and scandal that hung over Mary.

The angel's words underscore the miraculous nature of the virgin birth and the supernatural character surrounding the entire event of Christ's birth. It also provides divine assurance to Joseph (*"son of David"*) and to us that Jesus had legitimate royal lineage that legally came through Joseph as a descendant of King David. The angel's words provide the most irrefutable testimony to the essential truth of the virgin birth.

You can imagine how great Joseph's feelings of amazement, relief, and gratitude must have been once he realized what the Lord, through the heavenly messenger, had told him. Not only could he go ahead and take Mary as his wife with honor and righteousness, but he also could rejoice at the privilege of being allowed to bring up God's own Son.

Here we see the tremendous depth and firmness of Joseph's faith. When he awoke from the dream, he took Mary as his wife. They had the *huppa*, the wedding ceremony, and he spared her the shame, disgrace, and loneliness of having to bear the child alone and in anonymity. Joseph must have been a good man. Can you imagine the Almighty God of the universe depositing His only Son in the home of a man who wasn't?

Although to external appearances they were husband and wife, Joseph kept Mary a virgin until after Jesus was born (Matthew 1:25). Thus Isaiah's prophecy was literally fulfilled.

One popular legend has it that Mary remained a virgin the rest of her life. That's not true. After Jesus' birth Mary and Joseph had a normal physical relationship as husband and wife, and they produced at least six other children. The Bible even gives the names of some of Jesus' half–siblings (Matthew 13:55). Two of them wrote letters that are now in the Bible (James and Jude).

THE HUMAN AND DIVINE ANCESTRY OF CHRIST

Imagine having someone in your family who is none other than God in human flesh! Scripture tells us very little about Jesus' early life or family. We know that even at a young age, He was occupied with His Father's business (Luke 2:49). He clearly understood who He was and why He had come—to save His people from their sin.

When Jesus was older, He would . . .

- · Dwell among the sick to heal them.
- · Walk among the demon-possessed to liberate them.
- · Fellowship with the poor and downtrodden and needy.
- · Touch lepers to make them whole.
- · Minister to the hungry and destitute multitudes.
- · Feed and heal people in need.

But most of all He would seek and save the lost (Luke 19:10).

The ancestry of Jesus shows clearly how important God's grace was from generation to generation as the Father nurtured and protected the lineage He had chosen to give birth to the Messiah. Virtually every name in the list reveals some lesson about God's grace. Mankind's sin, rebellion, and treachery have utterly failed to thwart the grace of God.

Two genealogies in Scripture trace the lineage of Jesus (Matthew 1:1–17; Luke 3:23–38). Some people see these two lists as contradictory, but a close look shows they are not. Matthew starts with Abraham and follows the line through David to Jesus via Joseph's family, while Luke starts with Jesus and outlines the genealogy of Mary's family back through David and all the way back to Adam.

Matthew doesn't refer to Joseph as the father of Jesus, but as *"the husband of Mary, by whom Jesus was born"* (Matthew 1:16). Scripture is clear that Joseph was not the father of Jesus; God was. Because Jesus had no human father, He couldn't be a descendent of David except through His mother, but the legal right to rule always came through the father's side. This was true even in Jesus' case, because He was legally Joseph's oldest son. Thus we have two necessary genealogies. Luke shows that through Mary, Jesus was literally a blood descendent of David. Matthew proves through his adopted father, Joseph, that Jesus was legally in the royal line. In every way possible, He had the right to rule.

The fact that Jesus was the legal son of Joseph, but not his blood son, also fulfills another prophecy. The Davidic line of rulers had been cursed to end (Jeremiah 22:30), which seemed to contradict the Messiah promise. But through Joseph, Jesus inherited the legal right to David's throne without also inheriting the curse on David's biological heirs, starting with Jeconiah. His scriptural credentials are thorough, clear, and irrefutable. From every perspective, we can crown Jesus King of kings and Lord of lords.

How do we know that the genealogies were listed accurately? Because genealogies were vitally important in Hebrew culture. They determined the land one could own, rights of inheritance, basis of taxation, and who could be a priest. In the theocracy of

Israel—a kingdom ruled by God, with legal statutes about ancestral rights outlined in Scripture—genealogies were carefully maintained across the generations. If the religious leaders of the day wanted to refute Jesus' claim to be Messiah—and they certainly did—all they had to do was check the genealogies and tax records to see whether or not He had Davidic lineage, because only a son of David could be Messiah. On this point, their silence speaks volumes. The genealogies must be accurate. There was simply no denying our Lord's rightful ancestry and position of highest honor.

The
Truth
of the
Nativity

The story of the first Christmas is so beloved that singers and storytellers across the centuries have embellished and elaborated and mythologized the story in celebration. However, now most people don't know which details are biblical and which are fabricated. People usually imagine the manger scene with snow, singing angels, many worshipers, and a little drummer boy. None of that is found in the biblical account.

Christmas has become the product of an odd mixture of pagan ideas, superstition, fanciful legends, and plain ignorance. Let's try to sort it out. The place to begin is in God's Word, the Bible. Here we find not only the source of the original account of Christmas, but also God's commentary on it.

We can't know Jesus if we don't understand He is real. The story of His birth is no allegory. We dare not romanticize it or settle for a fanciful legend that renders the whole story meaningless. Mary and Joseph were real people. Their dilemma on finding no room at the inn surely was as frightening for them as it would be for you or me. The manger in which Mary laid Jesus must have reeked of animal smells. So did the shepherds, in all probability. That first Christmas was anything but picturesque.

But that makes it all the more wondrous. THAT BABY IN THE MANGER IS GOD! IMMANUEL!

That's the heart and soul of the Christmas message. There weren't many worshipers around the original manger—only a handful of shepherds. But one day every knee will bow before Him, and every tongue will confess He is Lord (Philippians 2:9–11). Those who doubt Him, those who are His enemies, those who merely ignore Him—all will one day bow, too, even if it be in judgment.

How much better to honor Him now with the worship He deserves! That's what Christmas ought to inspire.

WHO WAS IN THE STABLE?

Luke 2:7 sets the scene: "*[Mary] gave birth to her firstborn son; and she wrapped Him in cloths, and laid Him in a manger, because there was no room for them in the inn.*" That verse is explicitly concerned with a lonely birth. There were no midwives, no assistance to Mary at all. The Bible doesn't even mention that Joseph was present. Perhaps he was, but if he was typical of first–time fathers, he would have been of little help to Mary. She was basically on her own. Mary brought forth the child, *she* wrapped Him in swaddling cloths, and *she* laid Him in a manger. Where usually a midwife would clean the baby and wrap Him, there was no one. Mary did it herself. And where usually there would have been a cradle or basket for the baby, there was none. Mary had to put Him in an animal's feeding trough.

When Christ entered the world, He came to a place that had some of the smelliest, filthiest, and most uncomfortable conditions. But that is part of the wonder of divine grace, isn't it? When the Son of God came down from heaven, He came all the way down. He did not hang on to His equality with God; rather, He set it aside for a time and completely humbled Himself (Philippians 2:5–8).

WHO WERE THE SHEPHERDS?

In the same region there were some shepherds staying out in the fields and keeping watch over their flock by night. And an angel of the Lord suddenly stood before them, and the glory of the Lord shone around them; and they were terribly frightened. But the angel said to them, "Do not be afraid; for behold, I bring you good news of great joy which will be for all the people; for today in the city of David there has been born for you a Savior, who is Christ the Lord. This will be a sign for you: you will find a baby wrapped in cloths and lying in a manger." And suddenly there appeared with the angel a multitude of the heavenly host praising God and saying, "Glory to God in the highest, and on earth peace among men with whom He is pleased." When the angels had gone away from them into heaven, the shepherds began saying to one another, "Let us go straight to Bethlehem then, and see this thing that has happened which the Lord has made known to us." So they came in a hurry and found their way to Mary and Joseph, and the baby as He lay in the manger. When they had seen this, they made known the statement which had been told them about this Child. And all who heard it wondered at the things which were told them by the shepherds. But Mary treasured all these things, pondering them in her heart. The shepherds went back, glorifying and praising God for all that they had heard and seen, just as had been told them.

—LUKE 2:8–20

Out of the whole of Jerusalem society, God picked a band of shepherds to hear the news of Jesus' birth. This is intriguing because shepherds were among the lowest and most despised social groups. The very nature of their work kept them from entering into the mainstream of Israel's society. They couldn't maintain the ceremonial washings and observe all the religious festivals and feasts, yet these shepherds, just a few miles from Jerusalem, were undoubtedly caring for sheep that someday would be used as sacrifices in the temple. How fitting it is that they were the first to know of the Lamb of God!

More significantly, they came to see Him the night he was born. No one else did. Though the shepherds went back and told everyone what they had seen and heard, and though *"all who heard it wondered at the things which were told them by the shepherds"* (v. 18), not one other person came to see firsthand.

Scripture does not describe how the shepherds' search for the baby Jesus actually unfolded, but it's reasonable to assume that they entered Bethlehem and asked questions: "Does anybody know about a baby being born here in town tonight?" The shepherds might have knocked on several doors and seen other newborn babies before they found the special Child lying in the feeding trough. At that moment, those humble men knew for certain that the angels' announcement was a word from God. After their encounter with Joseph and Mary and Jesus, the shepherds couldn't help but tell others about what the angels had told them. They became, in effect, the first New Testament evangelists.

The shepherds' story is a good illustration of the Christian life. You first hear the revelation of the gospel and believe it (Romans 10:9–10). Then you pursue and embrace Christ. And having become a witness to your glorious conversion, you begin to tell others about it (Luke 2:17).

May God grant you the life–changing spiritual experiences and the ongoing attitude of enthusiasm and responsiveness that cause you to tell others that you, too, have seen Christ the Lord.

WHO WERE THE WISE MEN?

*I*n Matthew's account of Jesus' birth, we briefly meet a band of travelers who have mystified and fascinated Bible students for centuries:

> *Now after Jesus was born in Bethlehem of Judea in the days of Herod the king, magi from the east arrived in Jerusalem, saying, "Where is He who has been born King of the Jews? For we saw His star in the east and have come to worship Him." When Herod the king heard this, he was troubled, and all Jerusalem with him. Gathering together all the chief priests and scribes of the people, he inquired of them where the Messiah was to be born. They said to him, "In Bethlehem of Judea; for this is what has been written by the prophet: 'AND YOU, BETHLEHEM, LAND OF JUDAH, ARE BY NO MEANS LEAST AMONG THE LEADERS OF JUDAH; FOR OUT OF YOU SHALL COME FORTH A RULER WHO WILL SHEPHERD MY PEOPLE ISRAEL.'" Then Herod secretly called the magi and*

determined from them the exact time the star appeared. And he sent them to Bethlehem and said, "Go and search carefully for the Child; and when you have found Him, report to me, so that I too may come and worship Him." After hearing the king, they went their way; and the star, which they had seen in the east, went on before them until it came and stood over the place where the Child was. When they saw the star, they rejoiced exceedingly with great joy. After coming into the house they saw the Child with Mary His mother; and they fell to the ground and worshiped Him. Then, opening their treasures, they presented to Him gifts of gold, frankincense, and myrrh. And having been warned by God in a dream not to return to Herod, the magi left for their own country by another way.

—MATTHEW 2:1–12

The *magi*—called "wise men" in some versions of the Bible—seem to materialize out of nowhere. They just show up, leave their gifts, and disappear. We know almost nothing about them, but mythmakers have constructed numerous stories that most people accept as truth.

Myth

· Three kings came to Jesus in the stable the night He was born.

Facts

· We don't know the number of men, just the number of gifts.

· These magi, or wise men, probably were not kings.

· The magi found Jesus in a house.

· Their visit might have been weeks or months after His birth.

All manner of notions about the magi have been advanced. For instance, over the years, storytellers gave them the names Caspar, Balthasar, and Melchior, but none of that information was recorded. Also, tradition holds that one of them was an Ethiopian, but an Ethiopian would have had to travel from the south, not the east, to reach Bethlehem. We can, however, glean some general information about the magi from historical and biblical sources. What we discover is that the truth about these mysterious visitors may be even more peculiar than some of the legends.

The ancient Greek historian Herodotus records that the magi were a priestly caste of the Medes, a people who occupied the land where Iran is today. They were active throughout Babylon and Mesopotamia during much of the Old Testament era. The original magi were priests of the most ancient form of Zoroastrianism, a religion that is still practiced today in India by the Parsees.

The ancient world made little distinction between superstition and science. The science of astronomy was blended imperceptibly with the superstition of astrology. The magi were experts in both. They were occult practitioners. Our word *magic* comes from their name. They also were considered the scholars of their time—the wise men. No Persian could become king unless he mastered the scientific and religious discipline of the magi. Their teachings became known as *"the law of the Medes and the Persians"* (Esther 1:19; Daniel 6:8, 12, 15). It was seen as the highest code. And so in addition to being the oracles of their religion, they served as the scientists, mathematicians, philosophers, doctors, and legal authorities of their culture. Our word *magistrate* is another direct descendent of *magi*.

Magi are mentioned in the Old Testament. Jeremiah 39:3 refers to *"Nergal-sar-ezer the Rab-mag,"* or the chief magi in

Nebuchadnezzar's court. The magi of Nebuchadnezzar's court also are mentioned several times in Daniel (1:20; 2:2; 4:7; 5:11). That might be an important clue to understand how the magi of Jesus' day knew to anticipate His birth. The Hebrew captive Daniel made an early impression on Nebuchadnezzar by doing what the magi were supposed to be best at—interpreting a dream (Daniel 2). Because of this extraordinary miracle, Nebuchadnezzar made Daniel the master of the magi (v. 48). Daniel would have then become very influential among them, and because of his character and zeal for God, he almost certainly taught the magi about the true God and Jewish Scripture—including all the prophecies regarding the Messiah.

No one can know for sure how much Old Testament truth came into the magis' teaching, but there was ample opportunity for them to learn from Daniel and the other dispersed Jews. It seems evident that whatever truth from the Hebrews filtered into their system, much of it survived until the time of Christ. And so magi—who were familiar with Messianic prophecy and seeking the true God—found the One who had been born King of the Jews.

When magi from the east arrived in Jerusalem, King Herod was understandably troubled, because these influential men were going about the town asking for the One who had been born King of the Jews! Try to imagine the scene. These men probably arrived in Jerusalem with a great deal of pomp and show. Their typical costume would have included tall, cone–shaped hats like those we associate with wizards. They would have been riding not on camels, but more likely on Persian steeds or Arabian horses. They might even have been traveling with a small army, since their journey took them into foreign territory.

For their part, the magi must have assumed that everyone in Israel would know about the new King's birth and could tell them where He was. Imagine their surprise when they began asking people in Jerusalem, *"Where is He who has been born King of the Jews?"* (Matthew 2:2), and no one seemed to know what the magi were talking about!

We don't know how they knew the Messianic prophecies had been fulfilled, but obviously God revealed it to them in some way. He confirmed it with the sign of a star. Perhaps they drew the connection between that star and Numbers 24:17: *"A star shall come forth from Jacob, a scepter shall rise from Israel, and shall crush through the forehead of Moab, and tear down all the sons of Sheth."* Being astrologers, they would have been keenly interested in that verse. This is the only Old Testament verse that talks about a star being any kind of sign. And *"a scepter . . . from Israel"* does seem to suggest a king of the Jews. Perhaps they had figured that out. We are not told.

Every Christmas, the planetariums and astronomers offer explanations of the Christmas star. Some say it must have been Jupiter, or a comet, or the conjunction of two planets, or some other natural phenomenon. None of those explanations is plausible, because the star led the magi right to the house where Jesus was. No known natural occurrence could have done that.

So what was the star? No one knows, and Scripture doesn't say, but the biblical phenomenon that most closely resembles it is the *shekinah* glory, the visual expression of God's glory, which in the time of Moses led Israel to the Promised Land, appearing as a pillar of cloud by day and a pillar of fire by night (Exodus 13:21). It was the same glory that shone on the shepherds when they learned of

Christ's birth (Luke 2:9). Perhaps what the magi saw was a similar manifestation of God's glory, which appeared to them like a star.

Whatever that star was, it signified to them that Jesus had been born. After they left Herod, the star *"went on before them until it came and stood over the place where the Child was"* (Matthew 2:9).

The place where they found Jesus was not the stable where Jesus was born; instead, they found Him in a house (Matthew 2:11). This may have occurred months—even as much as two years—after Jesus' birth. Matthew says Herod ascertained from the magi when the star appeared (v. 7). Then when he learned they were not going to reveal Jesus' location to him, Herod *"became very enraged, and sent and slew all the male children who were in Bethlehem and all its vicinity, from two years old and under, according to the time which he had determined from the magi"* (v. 16). It's possible that Herod killed every child under two in the area just to make sure he had exterminated the infant King, but it's also possible that these events occurred that long after the birth of Christ.

It is significant that the magi worshiped when they found Jesus. Whatever their motives at the start of the journey, when they saw

Jesus, *"they fell to the ground and worshiped Him"* (v. 11). God in His grace opened their eyes to something His own people did not see—that Jesus was God in human form. From this response, it appears that they were converted and thus became the earliest Gentile believers in Christ.

The gifts of the magi had special significance. Gold and frankincense would be typical gifts for a king. Gold, the most precious metal then known to man, was a common symbol of royalty from the earliest times and remains so today. Frankincense, an expensive fragrance, had special significance in Old Testament worship (Leviticus 2:2). It was often sprinkled on offerings in the temple. The frankincense may therefore have had additional meaning in signifying Jesus' deity.

Myrrh, on the other hand, was an unusual gift for a newborn king. It was a substance used in embalming the dead (John 19:39). Mixed with wine, it had an anesthetic effect. When Jesus was crucified, He was offered a myrrh and wine mixture to drink, but He refused it (Mark 15:23). The gift of myrrh therefore seems to foreshadow Jesus' suffering and death. There's no indication that the magi foresaw the details of this. But it is likely that just as God guided the magi to the infant Jesus, He also guided them in the selection of gifts, so that the combination of gifts they brought would testify to the new King's royalty, His deity, and His death on behalf of humanity.

"Wise men still seek Him," the familiar phrase says. It's true. In all the world, there are only two kinds of people: those who are fools and those who are wise. Herod typifies one brand of fool, someone who overtly rejects the Savior. The Jewish religious leaders who counseled Herod were fools of a different kind. They didn't hate Jesus; they just didn't care about Him. They ignored Him. They were too busy and too wrapped up in themselves to bother with Him—just like most people today.

The magi, on the other hand, were true wise men. It wasn't convenient for them to come to Jesus, but they came anyway. Although it meant great sacrifice for them, they doggedly pursued until they found Him. They typify every true wise man or woman who has ever lived.

In Christ *"are hidden all the treasures of wisdom and knowledge"* (Colossians 2:3). May you be truly wise.

PEOPLE WHO MISSED CHRISTMAS

Nearly everyone missed that first Christmas. Like people today, they were busy, consumed with all kinds of things—some important, some not—but nearly everyone missed Christ. The similarities between their world and ours are striking. Every one of those people has a counterpart in modern society.

THE INNKEEPER

Scripture doesn't specifically mention him, but that night in Bethlehem, an innkeeper was confronted by a man and his pregnant wife. Not only did he turn Mary and Joseph away, but he apparently didn't even call for anyone to help a young mother about to give birth. The Son of God might have been born on his property. But he missed Christmas because he was so preoccupied. There is no indication that he was hostile or even unsympathetic. He was just busy, that's all. Millions of people today are consumed with activity—not necessarily sinful activity, just things that keep them busy. At Christmas, people are especially busy. Shopping, banquets, parties, concerts, school activities, and other things all compete for attention. And in the clutter of activity, many preoccupied people miss the Son of God.

HEROD

Herod pretended he wanted to worship Jesus Christ, but he was fearful of this One who was called King of the Jews. He didn't want any competition for his throne. His supremacy was in jeopardy. Today, many people won't allow anything to interfere with their career, position, power, ambition, plans, or lifestyle. They are not about to let someone else be king of their lives. They see Jesus as a threat, and so they miss Christmas. People don't mind taking time off work to commemorate Jesus' birth. They will even embrace Him as a resource when they get in trouble. They might gladly accept Him as a spiritual benefactor. They are even willing to add Him to their lives and call themselves Christians, but not if He insists on being King. They are as fearful and as jealous of losing their own self—determination as Herod was of losing his throne. They will guard at all costs their own priorities, values, and morals. The world is full of people who cry out, *"We do not want this man to reign over us"* (Luke 19:14). People want to chart their own destinies, and so we have a world of kings and queens who are not about to bow to Jesus Christ. Such people are governed by the same kind of jealous fear that drove Herod. Like him they miss Christmas.

THE RELIGIOUS LEADERS

A whole group of people who missed Christmas is mentioned in Matthew's account of Herod's treachery. They are the religious leaders (Matthew 2:4–6). They knew exactly where Christ was to be born, but they never bothered to walk the two miles to Bethlehem to find out for themselves if Messiah had indeed been born. Why did the religious leaders miss Christmas? Indifference. The religious leaders had all the facts. They just didn't care. They were self—righteous. They kept the law. They believed they were already all that God could ever ask of them. Indifference is a profound sin against Christ. Sadly, it is one of the most common reactions to Him. It is typical of religious people who don't think they need a Savior. Such people think they're all right just the way they are. That is a dangerous attitude. Jesus' primary ministry was to people who had problems and knew it. He said, *"I did not come to call the righteous, but sinners"* (Matthew 9:13). In other words, those who are indifferent—who don't realize they are sinners—cannot respond to His call. There may, in fact, be more people in the United States who ignore Christ because they don't understand their need for salvation. They don't openly oppose Him; they just ignore Him. They don't care about the remedy, because they don't believe they have the disease. Such people miss Christmas.

The Inhabitants of Jerusalem

Bethlehem is within easy walking distance of Jerusalem, and Jesus' birth was the fulfillment of all that the nation had hoped for. But the entire city missed it. Why? Because they were so busy with religious ritual that they missed the reality. They had abandoned the heart of their faith. Jesus didn't fit their system. They looked for a Messiah who would be a conquering hero, not a baby in a manger. They hoped for a leader who would support their religious system, but Jesus opposed everything it stood for. People like that are the hardest to reach with the good news of salvation. They are so determined to earn their own salvation, to prove they can be righteous on their own, that they cannot see the depth of their spiritual poverty. Religion can be a deadly trap. Rituals and rules enable people to feel spiritual when they are not. Religious activity is not synonymous with genuine righteousness. Religion will damn people to hell as surely as immorality. In fact, Scripture tells us Satan's ultimate trick is to disguise himself as an angel of light (2 Corinthians 11:14). And so he can use even religion to make people miss Christmas.

THE ROMANS

Jesus was born in the heyday of the Roman Empire. Roman soldiers must have been everywhere in Bethlehem and the surrounding area, overseeing the census, registering people, and keeping order. Yet they missed Jesus' birth. Why? Idolatry. They had their own gods—they were even willing to let their emperor pretend to be God. Christ did not fit into their pantheon. Paganism has a strong grip on our world today, and millions miss Christmas because of it. I'm not talking only about the dark paganism where Christ is unknown and where Christmas is unheard of. There is a subtler form of idolatry. Most people in North America don't worship carved idols or follow demonic superstition like the Romans did, but they nevertheless worship false gods. Some people worship money. Others worship sex. I know people who worship cars, boats, houses, power, prestige, popularity, and fame. Those things are pagan gods. Modern idolatry is selfishness and materialism. If you worship these things, you'll miss Christmas.

THE PEOPLE OF NAZARETH

Although Jesus was born in Bethlehem, He grew up in Nazareth and lived His perfect life before all the people there. Yet they completely overlooked Him. After years of living among these people, Jesus revealed to the Nazarenes that He was the Messiah (Luke 4:16–21). And what was their reaction? They tried to throw Him off a cliff (Luke 4:28–30)! That's what I call missing Christmas. The people of Nazareth, who should have known Him better than anyone, had no idea who He really was. Mark 6:6 says even Jesus wondered at their unbelief. What was their problem? Familiarity. They knew Him so well they couldn't believe He was anyone special. Familiarity mixed with unbelief is a deadly thing. Perhaps the most tragic sin of all is the unbelief of a person who has heard all the sermons, sat through all the Bible lessons, learned all the Christmas stories, but who still rejects Christ. There is no gospel, no good news for such a person, because he already knows and rejects the truth that could set him free (Hebrews 10:26–31). What a sad way to miss Christmas!

Perhaps you've been missing Christmas. You may receive presents, eat a big dinner, and decorate a tree, but you know in your heart that you are no different from the innkeeper, Herod, the religious leaders, the people of Jerusalem, the Romans, or the citizens of Nazareth. You are missing the reality of Christmas. You don't have to miss another one. Turn from your sin and unbelief and receive Christ as Lord and God. He will forgive your sin, change your life, and give you the greatest Christmas gift anyone can receive: Himself.

Don't miss Christmas this year!

The Fullness

of

Time

When the fullness of the time came, God sent forth His Son, born of a woman, born under the Law, so that He might redeem those who were under the Law, that we might receive the adoption as sons.

—GALATIANS 4:4–5

The first Christmas was perfectly timed. In God's sovereign timing, He ordered world events so everything was ready for Christ's coming and the subsequent outreach of the apostles. Looking back at the early church, we are amazed at how quickly the gospel spread in less than a century. The sovereign hand of God is clearly evident. Christ's advent could not have been timed more propitiously.

Politically, the Roman Empire was at its height. Rome had given the world good roads, a relatively fair system of government, and, most importantly, a degree of peace. For the first time in history, people could travel with relative ease almost anywhere in the empire—and the apostles could carry the gospel message to the uttermost parts of the world.

Culturally, the world was becoming more unified. More people than ever were being educated, and most of them knew Greek or Latin. Even the common people usually spoke Koine Greek, the dialect that the New Testament was written in.

Spiritually, the world was diverse, but open. Greek and Roman polytheism were gradually being replaced by rational and secular philosophies, or by emperor worship. Among the Jews, a renewed interest in the Scriptures was leading to a revival on the one hand, typified by the ministry of John the Baptist, and a strong pharisaic movement on the other. Christ could not have arrived at a more opportune time. It was the perfect time, sovereignly determined by God—"the fullness of time."

The Jewish people had been looking for their Messiah since Moses first prophesied that a great prophet would come (Deuteronomy 18:15). They were waiting eagerly for a deliverer. Particularly now that they lived under Roman oppression, the entire nation longed for His coming. He was the great hope of the ages. The destiny of

Israel was bound up in His coming. He was their deliverer, Messiah, Christ, the Anointed One. The intensity of their hunger is illustrated in the ministry of John the Baptist. People flocked to hear the one who had been sent to prepare the way for Messiah.

THE PERSON AND PURPOSE OF CHRIST

> *The angel said to her, "Do not be afraid, Mary; for you have found favor with God. And behold, you will conceive in your womb and bear a son, and shall name Him JESUS. He will be great and will be called the Son of the Most High, and the Lord God will give Him the throne of His father David. And He will reign over the house of Jacob forever, and His kingdom will have no end."*
>
> —LUKE 1:30–33

God's people had not seen or heard from an angel in more than four hundred years. During that time there had been no revelation from the Lord, no miracle, and certainly no sequence of miracles. But then for the second time in the span of a few months the same angel appeared, both times with an extraordinary birth announcement to an ordinary person. Gabriel is one of only two angels who are actually named in the Bible. The other one, Michael, is associated with assignments requiring power and strength (Revelation 12:7). Gabriel is God's supreme messenger who brought great, glorious, and crucial announcements from heaven. For example, he also delivered the pronouncement to Daniel regarding the future of redemptive history and the seventy–weeks prophecy (Daniel 9).

Gabriel delivered the most astounding and significant birth announcement ever. And it was even more incredible because he brought it directly from the throne of God. *"The angel answered and said to him, 'I am Gabriel, who stands in the presence of God, and I have been sent to speak to you and to bring you this good news'"* (Luke 1:19). This high–ranking angel of God came down out of heaven to an obscure Galilean town.

Everything about the angel's proclamation to Mary was divine. That God would send an angel with a message—and for the second time in less than a year (Luke 1:11–20)—was in itself amazing.

Gabriel's words about the divine child, Jesus, constitute a summary of the entire person and work of our Lord and Savior. The summation appears rather simple on the surface, but the complexity of each facet challenges our ability to grasp and appreciate all that the angel said to Mary. It is truly awesome to contemplate Jesus' saving work, His perfectly righteous life, His title of deity, and His kingly position—all in the same concise overview.

JESUS' SAVING WORK

First, the angel gives a preliminary indication of the Child's saving mission. Jesus' name itself comes from the Hebrew *Yeshua*, which means "Jehovah saves" (Matthew 1:21). The God of the Old Testament was a saving God, and His people knew it (2 Samuel 7:23; Job 19:25; Isaiah 44:21–23; 45:21; Hosea 14:2; Joel 2:12–13; Jonah 2:9). Later in Luke's description of the incarnation, he reiterates and underscores the point that the Child, Jesus, was the long-awaited Savior: *"For there is born to you this day in the city of David a Savior, who is Christ the Lord'"* (2:11 NKJV); *"For my*

[Simeon's] eyes have seen Your salvation'" (2:30); "And coming in that instant she [Anna] gave thanks to the Lord, and spoke of Him to all those who looked for redemption in Jerusalem" (2:38 N K J V). And later in his Gospel, while chronicling Christ's ministry in Perea, Luke conveyed in Jesus' own words the reason He came: "'for the Son of Man has come to seek and to save that which was lost'" (19:10).

JESUS' PERFECTLY RIGHTEOUS LIFE

Gabriel makes the simple statement that Jesus would be "great." Some commentators would say it's better to translate the Greek word for "great" as *extraordinary*. Or it might be better still to substitute the adjective *splendid, magnificent, noble, distinguished, powerful*, or *eminent*. But those words still don't allow us to speak as excitedly as we ought about the life of Jesus. Christ's greatness is best understood in relation to what the apostle John wrote about Him.

> But although He had done so many signs before them, they did not believe in Him, that the word of Isaiah the prophet might be fulfilled, which he spoke:

"Lord, who has believed our report?
And to whom has the arm of the LORD *been revealed?"*
Therefore they could not believe, because Isaiah said again:
"He has blinded their eyes and hardened their hearts,
Lest they should see with their eyes,
Lest they should understand with their hearts and turn,
So that I should heal them."
These things Isaiah said when he saw His glory and spoke of Him.

—JOHN 12:37–41 NKJV

John's second quotation from the prophet is from Isaiah 6:9–10, when Isaiah witnessed God's glory in the temple and spoke about Him. Isaiah saw the glory (or greatness) of Christ at the same time he saw the glory of God, because the glory of Christ is the same as the glory of God. The prophet Isaiah knew that one day God would send the Messiah, His Son, to live a perfect life among His people and to save them from their sins (Isaiah 7:14; 9:6–7; 53:4–6). He had a preview of the same glory of Christ that the apostles later witnessed and described (Matthew 17:1–8; John 1:14). When Gabriel told Mary that Jesus would be great, he meant that Jesus would manifest the very glory of God.

Jesus' Title of Deity

Gabriel's announcement also affirms the deity of Christ. "*[He] will be called the Son of the Most High.*" "Most High" was simply a title for God, clearly indicating that nobody is higher than He is. Mary and other righteous Jews were familiar with that title because it is used throughout the Old Testament (see Genesis 14:18, Psalm 47:2, Psalm 91:1, Daniel 7:18). The Hebrew equivalent of the Greek term used by Luke is *El Elyon*, "God Most High." This title refers to God's sovereignty and the fact that no one is higher, more exalted, or more powerful than He is. To identify Jesus as the Son of the Most High is to declare that He has the same essence as the Most High God. "*He is the radiance of His glory and the exact representation of His nature, and upholds all things by the word of His power. When He had made purification of sins, He sat down at the right hand of the Majesty on high*" (Hebrews 1:3). Jesus told His disciples, "'*He who has seen Me has seen the Father*'" (John 14:9). And He boldly asserted to His opponents, "'*I and the Father are one*'" (John 10:30). Gabriel announced, and the New Testament confirms, that Jesus unquestionably was and is worthy of His divine title, because He truly is the Son of God.

JESUS' KINGLY POSITION

The story of Jesus will wonderfully conclude with His sovereign rule over earth and heaven. The story of redemption will culminate with great precision in the glorious reign of Jesus Christ on David's throne over the nation of Israel, by which He will establish an earthly Kingdom for a thousand years, followed by an eternal Kingdom.

When Jesus came to earth as an infant, He came with the proper credentials to rule. He offered His Kingdom to His people, but they spurned it and then rejected and executed Him. However, Christ will return in glory and with omnipotence to establish His Kingdom (Revelation 19:1–21:8).

The Old Testament writers, under the inspiration of the Holy Spirit, foresaw the coming of Christ's Kingdom. For example,

David writes, "*Yet I have set My King on My holy hill of Zion. I will declare the decree: the LORD has said to Me, 'You are My Son. Today I have begotten You. Ask of Me, and I will give You the nations for your inheritance, and the ends of the earth for Your possession'*" (Psalm 2:6–8 NKJV). In 2 Samuel 7:12–16, God told David he would have a Son who would reign forever. And that Son was not Solomon, but the Messiah, Jesus.

The Bible promises that all believers will be part of God's Kingdom. Even though God will take us to heaven through death or the Rapture, He will include us in the millennial Kingdom. Others will be saved during the Tribulation and become members of the Kingdom. Christ will return, kill the unbelieving, and then establish His earthly Kingdom of righteousness, peace, and truth. And once the final rebellion of Satan and his followers is crushed and they're sent to the Lake of Fire, the Lord will establish His eternal Kingdom. The magnificent words of Handel's "Hallelujah Chorus" perfectly describe the conclusion: "He shall reign forever and ever!"

Hallelujah!

And He was handed the book of the prophet Isaiah. And when He had opened the book, He found the place where it was written:

"The Spirit of the LORD is upon Me,
Because He has anointed Me
To preach the gospel to the poor;
He has sent Me to heal the brokenhearted,
To proclaim liberty to the captives
And recovery of sight to the blind,
To set at liberty those who are oppressed;
To proclaim the acceptable year of the LORD."

Then He closed the book, and gave it back to the attendant and sat down. And the eyes of all who were in the synagogue were fixed on Him. And He began to say to them, "Today this Scripture is fulfilled in your hearing."

—*Luke 4:17–21*

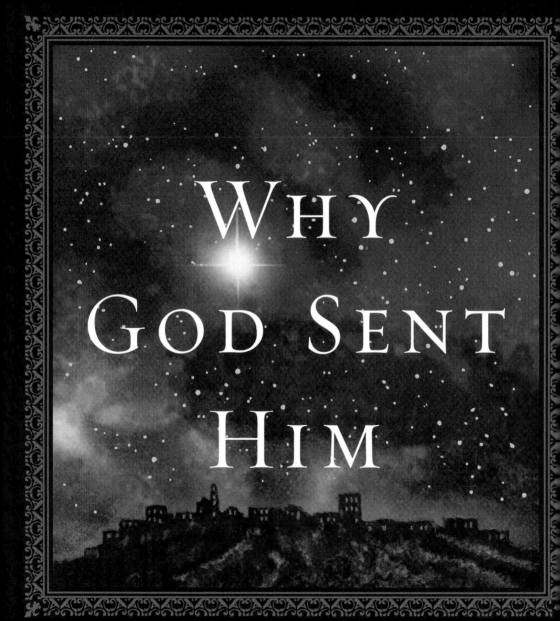

WHY
GOD SENT
HIM

On that very first Christmas, earth was oblivious to all that was happening. But heaven wasn't. The holy angels were waiting in anticipation to break forth in praise and worship and adoration at the birth of the newborn Child. This Child's birth meant deliverance for mankind. The angel told Joseph: *"He will save His people from their sins"* (Matthew 1:21). Jesus knew that to do that, He would have to die.

The important issue of Christmas is not so much that Jesus came, but why He came. There was no salvation in His birth. Nor did the sinless way He lived His life have any redemptive force of its own. His example, flawless as it was, could not rescue us from our sins. Even His teaching, the greatest truth ever revealed, could not save us. There was a price to be paid for our sins. Someone had to die. Only Jesus could do it.

Hebrews 10:5–7 gives us a remarkable look at the heart of the Savior before His birth. He knew He was entering the world to be the final and ultimate sacrifice for sin. His body had been divinely prepared by God specifically for that purpose. Jesus was going to die for the sins of the world, and He knew it. Moreover, He was doing it willingly. That was the whole point of the Incarnation.

Jesus came to earth to reveal God to mankind. He came to teach truth. He came to fulfill the Law. He came to offer His kingdom. He came to show us how to live. He came to reveal God's love. He came to bring peace. He came to heal the sick. He came to minister to the needy.

But all those reasons are incidental to His ultimate purpose. He could have done them all without being born as a human. He could have simply appeared—like the angel of the Lord often did in the Old Testament—and accomplished everything in the above list, without literally becoming a man. But He had one more reason for coming: He came to die.

Here's a side to the Christmas story that isn't often told. Those soft little hands, fashioned by the Holy Spirit in Mary's womb, were made so that nails might be driven through them. Those baby feet, pink and unable to walk, would one day walk up a dusty hill to be nailed to a cross. That sweet infant's head with sparkling eyes and eager mouth was formed so that someday men might force a crown of thorns onto it. That tender body, warm and soft, wrapped in swaddling cloths, would one day be ripped open by a spear.

Jesus was born to die.

Don't think I'm trying to put a damper on your Christmas spirit. Far from it—for Jesus' death, though devised and carried out by men with evil intentions, was not a tragedy. In fact, it represents the greatest victory over evil anyone has ever accomplished. There are several reasons for that, all summed up in Hebrews 2:9–18.

HE BECAME A SUBSTITUTE FOR US

We do see Him who was made for a little while lower than the angels, namely, Jesus, because of the suffering of death crowned with glory and honor, so that by the grace of God He might taste death for everyone.

—HEBREWS 2:9

Jesus died as our substitute. He was the One who created the angels. But in His incarnation, our Lord made Himself lower than them. This does not mean that He became less than God or that He gave up any aspect of His deity. *"For a little while"* He stepped down to a level that was lower than the angels. In what sense was He lower than the angels? *"Because of the suffering of death crowned with glory and honor."* No angel could ever die. Death is reserved for mortals, and Jesus had to die.

For what reason? *"That by the grace of God He might taste death for everyone."* He was our substitute. When He was nailed on the cross, He died for you and He died for me. He died for everyone who would believe.

That's what we call the grace of God. He didn't come because we asked for or deserved His intervention, but because He is a God of grace. His lovingkindness toward us is absolutely undeserved. Christ chose to die for us solely on the basis of His sovereign goodwill.

HE PIONEERED OUR SALVATION

For it was fitting for Him, for whom are all things, and through whom are all things, in bringing many sons to glory, to perfect the author of their salvation through sufferings.

—HEBREWS 2:10

Jesus' death was what made it possible for Him to pioneer our salvation. In Hebrews 2:10, the word translated "author" means *pioneer*, *leader*, or *trailblazer*. It refers to someone who starts something for others to follow. The word could refer to the founder of a city or to the leader of an exploration. It cannot refer to someone who stands at the rear and issues orders. And it cannot refer to someone who follows a path that has already been laid out.

Christ is the first and only initiator of salvation. There is no way to get to God apart from Him. Jesus said, *"I am the way, and the truth, and the life; no one comes to the Father but through Me"* (John 14:6). Scripture is clear; there is only one path to God, and Jesus is the trailblazer: *"There is salvation in no one else; for there is no other name under heaven that has been given among men by which we must be saved"* (Acts 4:12).

HE SANCTIFIED HIS PEOPLE

For both He who sanctifies and those who are sanctified are all from one Father; for which reason He is not ashamed to call them brethren, saying, "I WILL PROCLAIM YOUR NAME TO MY BRETHREN, IN THE MIDST OF THE CONGREGATION I WILL SING YOUR PRAISE." *And again,* "I WILL PUT MY TRUST IN HIM." *And again,* "BEHOLD, I AND THE CHILDREN WHOM GOD HAS GIVEN ME."

—HEBREWS 2:11–13

"Sanctify" means *set apart* or *make holy*. This passage is saying that Jesus Christ is holy, and that He is capable of making us holy.

Perhaps the greatest theological dilemma of all time was resolved at the cross. It was the question of how a holy God could communicate mercy and grace to sinful people. Sin demands death. Yet God's lovingkindness and mercy are never ending. He loves sinners. If he simply accepted us as we are and ignored our sin, His own holiness would be tainted. Christ resolved the question by taking our punishment on Himself. He brought mercy and justice together at the cross—and satisfied the demands of both.

How many of our sins did He pay for? All of them. The ones in the past, the ones in the future, all of them. Thus He can righteously deal with us as if we were sinless. He has declared us holy. He makes us as holy and spotless as sinless creatures (Ephesians 1:4; 5:27; Colossians 1:22).

We are not sinless in practice, but part of Christ's sanctifying work is the transformation of our desires and actions (2 Corinthians 5:17; Galatians 5:24; Titus 2:12). He is conforming us to His image, sanctifying even our behavior (Romans 8:29; 2 Corinthians 3:18; Ephesians 4:24). He's making us more and more like Himself.

The holiness with which He sanctifies us cannot be marred. *"For by one offering He has perfected for all time those who are sanctified"* (Hebrews 10:14). Once we have received the imputed holiness of Jesus Christ, nothing in this universe can take it away. Christ paid the penalty for sin in full, and our sins can never be brought up against us (Romans 8:33). No one—not even the accuser, Satan— can recall our sins to use them against us.

HE CONQUERED SATAN

Therefore, since the children share in flesh and blood, He Himself likewise also partook of the same, that through death He might render powerless him who had the power of death, that is, the devil, and might free those who through fear of death were subject to slavery all their lives.

—HEBREWS 2:14–15

Did you realize that one of the main reasons for the incarnation was so Christ could deliver a death blow to Satan? The first prophecy ever given about Jesus foretold that He would crush the serpent's head (Genesis 3:15). Here, in the New Testament, is the proclamation that the ancient prophecy was fulfilled.

Satan's great power is death. He is the paymaster for the wages of sin. If He can keep a person living in sin until death, he's got that person forever. Someone had to conquer death to destroy Satan's weapon, and that's exactly what Jesus did. He came out of the grave, exploded out of the shackles of death, and announced, *"Because I live, you will live also"* (John 14:19). And so we say, *"O death, where is your victory? O death, where is your sting?"* (1 Corinthians 15:55).

HE BECAME OUR PERFECT HIGH PRIEST

Therefore, He had to be made like His brethren in all things, so that He might become a merciful and faithful high priest in things pertaining to God, to make propitiation for the sins of the people. For since He Himself was tempted in that which He has suffered, He is able to come to the aid of those who are tempted.

—HEBREWS 2:17–18

That is one of the most remarkable passages in all of Scripture. What can it possibly mean? That He learned something in His incarnation He did not know before? No. There has never been anything He did not know. It was not a question of His gaining some knowledge or experience He needed.

But to be a sympathetic high priest, Christ had to be a man. A high priest is a mediator between men and God. Obviously, a high priest would have to understand to some degree the mind of God and also the mind of man. And the perfect high priest would be someone who was both God and man. That's exactly who Jesus Christ is—the perfect mediator.

"*We do not have a high priest who cannot sympathize with our weaknesses*" (Hebrews 4:15). He was hungry. He was thirsty. He was overcome with fatigue. He slept. He grew. He loved. He was astonished. He marveled. He was glad. He grieved. He became angry. He was troubled. He read the Scripture. He prayed all night. He wept. He is one of us in every sense—the perfect sympathizer.

And He is God—the perfect high priest.

God is justifiably angry with humanity's sin. Yet He loves us enough that He gave His own Son to live on earth, die on a cross, and bear our sins in His own body, suffering the full weight of God's wrath, which should have been our punishment. He paid our penalty and restored peace between us and God. It could not have been accomplished any other way.

THE GIFT OF GOD

Christmas is first of all a celebration of God's love toward man. The babe in the manger is more than just a tender child. He is the image of God, the *prototokos*. He took on a body of human flesh so that he might bear in that body the sins of the world. He made possible the gift of God—eternal life (Romans 6:23). That is the sum of the Christmas message.

Don't get lost in the scope of it all. The incarnation of God in Jesus Christ is nothing if it is not personal. God loves you, individually. He knows you better than you know yourself, yet He loves you. He entered this world, took on human flesh, and died on a cross to bear your sin, to pay the penalty for your iniquity, to remove your guilt. He did it so that you might enter into His presence.

You must respond.

He calls you to respond in faith. Turn from your sin to Him. *"The Lord is not slow about His promise [to judge the earth] . . . but is patient toward you, not wishing for any to perish but for all to come to repentance"* (2 Peter 3:9).

Believe Him, and trust Him with your life. *"He who believes in the Son has eternal life; but he who does not obey the Son will not see life, but the wrath of God abides on him"* (John 3:36). He who created everything will make you a new creature, remolded in His image, with new desires and a new heart. *"Therefore if anyone is in Christ, he is a new creature; the old things passed away; behold, new things have come"* (2 Corinthians 5:17). Your life will never be the same.

And this Christmas will truly be a time to celebrate, for you will have the greatest gift you can ever receive, *"being justified as a gift by His grace through the redemption which is in Christ Jesus"* (Romans 3:24).

Take another look at the manger this Christmas. Look beyond the tender scene and see what Jesus Himself knew even before He came—that He was born to die.

He died for you. He bore your sin. He purchased your salvation. He guaranteed your sanctification. He destroyed your enemy. And He became a sympathetic high priest. Even as you read this, He is seated next to the Father in heaven, ready to make intercession for you (Hebrews 7:25).

This is God's gift to you.

ABOUT THE AUTHOR

John MacArthur, one of today's foremost Bible teachers, is the author of numerous bestselling books that have touched millions of lives. He is pastor–teacher of Grace Community Church in Sun Valley, California, and president of The Master's College and Seminary. He is also president of Grace to You, the ministry that produces the internationally syndicated radio program *Grace to You* and a host of print, audio, and Internet resources—all featuring John's popular verse–by–verse teaching. He also authored the notes in *The MacArthur Study Bible*, which has been awarded the Gold Medallion and has sold more than 500,000 copies. John and his wife, Patricia, have four children (all married), who have given them thirteen grandchildren.

For more information about John MacArthur and his Bible–teaching resources, contact Grace to You at:

800–55–GRACE   or   www.gty.org
(800–554–7223)